CREATIVE BONE

easy
Decorating
Projects

CAROL FIELD DAHLSTROM

even if you don't have a

creative bone

in your body!

or even if you do!

Carol Field Dahlstrom
Brave Ink Press
Ankeny, Iowa

Author and Editor
Carol Field Dahlstrom

Book Design
Lyne Neymeyer

Photography
Dean Tanner— Primary Image, Lyne Neymeyer, Pete Krumhardt

How-to Illustrations: Kristen Krumhardt
Copy Editing: Jill Philby
Proofreading: Elizabeth Dahlstrom
Props and Location: Roger Dahlstrom
Technical Assistant: Judy Bailey
Special thanks to these people for helping to create some of the projects and gathering information for this book: Donna Chesnut, Ardith Field, Maryanna Lanigan, Carol McGarvey, Jan Temeyer

ISBN 0-9768446-0-5
Library of Congress Control Number: 2005909519

Separations: Scan Graphics, Des Moines, Iowa
Printed in the United States of America
First Edition   Second Printing

While all of the information has been checked and tested, human error can occur.
Carol Field Dahlstrom, Inc. and Brave Ink Press cannot be held responsible for any loss or injury associated with the making of any project or information in this book.

Carol Field Dahlstrom, Inc. and Brave Ink Press strive to provide high quality products and information that will make your life happier and more beautiful. Please write or e-mail us with your comments, questions, and suggestions or to inquire about purchasing books at braveink@aol.com or Brave Ink Press, P.O. Box 663, Ankeny, Iowa 50021.

Visit us at www.braveink.com to see upcoming books from Brave Ink Press or to purchase books.

The "I can do that" books™

Your Decorating Style?
Easy Style!

We all want to have our homes be comfortable and beautiful places for our families, friends, and ourselves. And we want our style to be creative, personal—and easy.

In this book we've taken the mystery out of making decorating projects for your home. We show you how to decorate with many of the things you already have in your home by simply rearranging them. We give you inspiration and ideas for creating simple and easy projects that you can make in minutes. And when we show you a new technique, we give you easy-to-follow directions and down-to-earth illustrations.

So even if you don't have a creative bone in your body (or even if you do!), you can find, arrange, create, and enjoy decorating your home in your own easy style. There is no doubt that soon you'll be saying, "I can do that!"

Carol Field Dahlstrom

easy decorating projects

even if you don't have a

creative bone

in your body!

How to Use this Book

Decorating should be easy and fun and should reflect your own personal style. We know how busy you are, so in this book we give you hundreds of ideas that you can do in very little time.

We show you easy and clever project ideas in three ways: With our **before and after** photos, you will be inspired to find the things you need and then arrange or create the project you want. Many of the things you

Sometimes we show you a **before and after** photo so you'll know exactly how the decorating project was made. You'll be surprised at just how few things it takes to make the decorating statement you want to make.

Many of the projects in the book you can **make in minutes**. These projects give you the photo and idea together so you have the information you need to create just the decorating project you want in very little time.

may already have in your home and just need to gather them together.

Our **make in minutes** photos will inspire you to show your own decorating style and you'll find that it only takes a little time.

And our **make it easy** projects will teach you something you'll love to learn. With accurate step-by-step instructions, you are sure to succeed. So go ahead and get started—its time to show your own creative decorating style!

It is always fun to learn something new. We **make it easy** by showing you some great ideas and then give you step-by-step illustrations so your project will turn out perfectly every time.

If you need special stitches or a pattern to complete your decorating project, you'll find that in the book, too. It's all here just for you.

decorating with flowers

Whether you are arranging them in fancy

vases or simple canning jars, floating them in

glittered water, or tucking them into a

glorious wreath, flowers are a natural choice

when it comes to decorating. So take a deep

breath and get ready for the loveliness that

flowers can bring to your decorating style.

Before and After
Marbleized Florals

Find it! Choose a container that suits the kind of flowers that you want to showcase. Because our day lilies are a casual flower, we chose a large glass canning jar to hold the arrangement. Then find marbles that share the colors that your flowers have. Find a fabric in the same hues to set off the arrangement.

Arrange it! Begin your arrangement by adding about 1 cup of water to the bottom of the vase. Add a shallow layer of marbles and then add the cut flowers. Fill the jar with water and then add the rest of the marbles until you like the marble height. Adjust the flowers and place the arrangement on the fabric.

Start with marbles in colors
that you love or flowers that
grow in the colors you love—
then combine them to make a
most lovely marbleized look.

Make it Easy

Good Idea Choose the same flower type in three shades of color and place them in three vases of the same color—but not necessarily the same style. This ultra-simple arrangement will sit nicely on a window sill or on a glass-topped coffee table.

Shades of Color Beautiful roses in shades that you love make a strong statement when they are grouped from light to dark or from shade to shade. Purchase a few flowers in each shade of the same color family and then arrange them in a bowl that has a grid so they fill the bowl to the brim.

Gridded Bowl Vase

What you need
- **Bowl for holding flowers**
- **Pencil**
- **Green (or black) electrical tape**
- **Ruler**
- **Scissors**

What you do

1. Depending upon the size of the bowl that you are using and the number of flowers that you want to use, plan how many grids you will need. Mark dots across from each other with the pencil. Cut the electrical tape two inches longer that the diameter of the bowl and stretch the pieces across the bowl matching up the marks made with the pencil. Trim off the excess tape leaving only about ½-inch of tape coming down over the side of the bowl.

2. Use the pencil to mark dots on the opposite side of the bowl. Overlap the pieces of tape in the same way, stretching the tape to fit securely over the bowl.

3. Add water to the bowl. Cut the flowers so the stems are just long enough to fit into the bowl and will touch the water. Arrange the flowers from light to dark grouping more than one flower in each gridded hole if necessary. The flowers should come down over the top of the bowl to cover the tape. Adjust the flowers as you like.

Make in Minutes

Candlestick Vases
Flowers can fit into so many lovely containers. Candlesticks, turned upside down, make dainty holders for lovely little flowers. Choose candlesticks that have hollow bases and group them using a variety of heights and shapes. In no time you'll have a sparkling floral arrangement.

Nature's Colors Use the surprises that nature gives you to inspire your decorating. Look closely and you'll see a little stripe of red in these pretty purple tulips. Arrange the tulips in a bowl that reflects that unexpected red color and then set it on a red object to bring out the color even more. For tips on arranging flowers in bowls, see page 15.

Before and After
Old Fashioned Beauties

Find it! Look for a vintage item in your home that may not be intended to be a flower container. Then add a simple glass vase or tumbler inside the container to hold some real beauties. Find some twigs in the backyard and even some whole coffee beans to give the arrangement a new flavor.

Arrange it! Place the glass or vase in the upright container. It is best if the top of the glass is lower than the can or container. Fill the glass half full with water. Arrange the flowers in the glass. (See page 35 for tips on arranging flowers.) Add the twigs to the arrangement. Add a few whole coffee beans around the bottom of the arrangement if you like. Sit back and smell the lovely aromas.

When using flowers as your decorating stars, show them off in unexpected containers. A vintage coffee can with aged colors compliments the wonderful reds of these old-fashioned beauties.

Make in Minutes

Floating Posies One of the easiest and most lovely ways to present pretty blooms is to float the flower heads in water. Choose a container or bowl that is not too deep and fill it with water. Pick flowers that are all about the same size, snip just the tops off, and gently place them in the water. The flowers will last for several days.

Pretty Preservation Iron pieces with hooks can be purchased at gift shops or at home centers. Paint the piece the color you want and then hang it inside or out to display flowers as you dry them. Choose flowers that have stems that will naturally hang over the hooks. Hang the flowers at different levels for interest.

21

Before and After
Floral Wreath

Find it! Making a pretty floral wreath is really very easy. Purchase a floral foam wreath form from a crafts or floral supply store. Then choose the flowers that you love. Many kinds of flowers will work for the wreath, but flowers with full blooms that are close to the stem work the best.

Arrange it! Submerge and soak the form in a bowl of water for at least an hour. Remove the form and place on a plate or tray. Cut the blooms from the flowers and stick into the form until covered. After the wreath is covered with the flower heads, place it on a plate or cake stand. Use the wreath as a centerpiece to showcase favorite dishes or to surround a candle. The water in the foam will keep the wreath fresh for days.

Glorious blooms gather
together to create a
stunning wreath of color
and texture.

Make in Minutes

Floral Inspiration Use the pattern from a
favorite cup or mug to be the inspiration for your
floral container. These delicate coffee mugs have
beautiful color and a rich floral pattern. The flowers in
the mugs match the color palette of the containers.
Little teacups with pretty patterns also work well for
this oh-so-easy idea.

24

In a Row Use three vases or containers that are the same size and shape to showcase beautiful blooms. Arrange the flowers in the vases in a similar way and then place the vases in a row on a harvest table or area that allows for length. For tips on arranging flowers, see page 35.

In the Box

Sometimes the simplest is the best. Choose a weathered wooden piece—old or new—to fill with flowers and set outside. We have chosen a vintage tool box that was painted with a blue wash. Select flowers in the same color tones that coordinate with the container just as we have done with our pretty pansies. If you choose the flowers first, paint the container in a tone to match the flowers. Plant the flowers in small plastic flower containers and set inside the box. Because the flowers are in small containers, water them often to keep them fresh.

Before and After
Asian Influence

Find it!   A large brandy snifter vase purchased at a crafts or discount store serves as the holder for this striking arrangement. The glass to hold the water inside can be a tumbler or small vase. Choose a flower variety that reflects the Asian influence such as birds of paradise. Fortune cookies can be purchased inexpensively at Asian food stores.

Arrange it!   Set the smaller vase inside the brandy snifter making sure that there is plenty of space between the glasses for the fortune cookies. Cut the flower stems to measure about 1½ times the height of the brandy snifter. Fill the inside container with water and add the flowers. Carefully place the fortune cookies between the vases.

Lucky you! What fun you'll have creating this clever centerpiece of fresh flowers and amazing good fortune.

For more ideas using two vases and tips on filling the space, turn the page.

Make it Easy

Vase Disguises

A small vase inside a larger vase or a small tumbler inside a larger tumbler is a clever way to create your own unique way of displaying flowers. Choose sets of holders that fit inside one another with enough room between the pieces to hold little objects to add color, texture, and a bit of surprise to the arrangement. For tips on filling the outside vase, see opposite.

Vase Disguise

What you need
- Tracing paper
- Funnel pattern from page 156
- Pencil
- Scissors
- Printer paper or lightweight cardboard
- One small vase or tumbler
- One large vase or tumbler
- Colorful or textured items small enough to fit between the two vases or tumbler
- Skewer or toothpick

What you do

Trace around the paper funnel pattern on page 156 being sure to mark all lines. Cut out. Trace around the pattern onto the printer paper or lightweight cardboard and cut out. Line up the dotted lines and staple together. You just made a paper funnel.

1. Place the small vase or tumbler inside the large vase or tumbler.

2. Hold the paper funnel between the two vases or tumblers and pour the small items between the containers.

3. Use a skewer or toothpick to arrange the items between the containers. Fill the inside tumbler or vase with flowers and water. Oh, how pretty.

In a Row

Pretty blooms need nothing more than simple

containers to hold them if you display them in

a row. Choose flowers that fit the same mood as

the containers. We chose country daisies that

naturally fit in the canning jar containers.

The containers are in varying sizes and heights

to add interest to the arrangement. We placed

the row of flowers on a well-worn dresser to

create a feeling of warmth and country charm.

Simple Glossary

Here are some terms that will be helpful to know when you are decorating with flowers.

Florist's Foam:
A soft, often green, foam used to hold flowers in a vase or container. The foam is soaked in water before the flowers are arranged.

Floral Tubes:
Small plastic or glass tubes designed for holding water for a single flower.

Floral Frog:
Any type of pronged, wire, or glass holder that is designed to hold flowers in a vase or a vessel.

Rose Bowl:
A small bowl-shaped container that is designed to hold water and floating flower blooms.

Floral Tape:
Green tape that stretches when used. This tape is especially designed for use in floral arrangements.

Annuals:
Flower or plant varieties that need to be planted every year to bloom.

Perennials:
Flowers or plant varieties that bloom for many seasons after being planted the first year.

Cleaning:
A florist's term for removing the thorns from roses or other thorned varieties of flowers.

Quick Takes

- With so many choices, it's easy to pick flowers you love for your home. Fancy is not necessary. Gather posies from your garden or from the grocery store. Choose what makes you feel good.

- Look around your home. Don't pick the first vase on the shelf. Instead, choose interesting containers, such as a teapot, a tall glass, old canning jar, or a white ironstone pitcher. Any container that holds water is a potential choice.

- Treat yourself well. Just for fun, put a single stem in a short bud vase on your kitchen window sill.

- Instead of a huge centerpiece when you host a brunch or dinner, place a mini bud vase at each guest's spot for their own personal posy. They'll love the gesture, and your table will look stunning and filled with flowers.

- Give yourself a good start in the morning. How about a small bouquet on your bedside table or on the bathroom vanity for a punch of color to get you moving?

- When ordering from a florist, take in a special container that you like from home. That way, your arrangement will make a personal statement.

- Branch out. Don't just display flowers. Take a walk. There are lots of interesting grasses, berries, and leaves to make an arrangement.

- The rules for arranging flowers are few. If you want to follow standard flower arranging rules, try not to have the flowers too top-heavy in the vase. If the flowers are more than 1¼ times the height of the vase, it may seem like the vase will tip over and the look will not be pleasing. Choose blooms that fit the size of the vase. For example, if you are using a small cup for a vase, choose tiny blooms with thin stems.

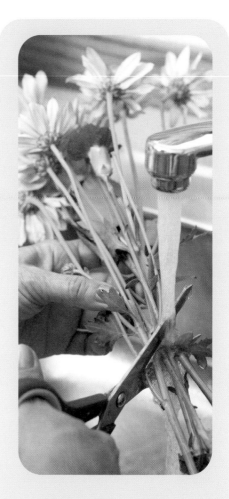

- To keep blooms fresher longer, cut the flower stems at an angle and under running water before putting them into the vase or container. After cutting, put the cut flowers immediately into the container of water.

decorating with dishes

It's fun to decorate with all kinds of dishes

because of their unlimited colors, unusual

and fun shapes, and amazing accessibility.

Stack them, line them up, fill them with flowers,

or nestle them in a bowl—dishes are ready and

waiting to help you decorate with ease.

Before and After
Bowl of Dishes

Find it! Antique ironstone or your favorite contemporary dishes—whatever you have and love to look at—is perfect to display in a large wooden bowl. Add some small items such as nuts in shells to fill in the spaces and add even more interest and texture.

Arrange it! Start by placing the large plates in the back of the bowl and then layering the dishes in the bowl with the cups in the front. Amazingly, the dishes are easy to arrange and will nestle together nicely. Add little pieces of paper toweling between and under the individual dishes if they slide too much. Add the nuts around the finished arrangement if you like.

All cuddled together in a warm wooden bowl, dishes are a lovely decorating statement all by themselves.

Make in Minutes

Color Compatible What could be easier than
to find the perfect dish in the color and style that you
love and then fill it with natural things that are nearly
the same color? This monochromatic look can be
achieved using most any single color tone dish and
filling it with a variety of things including fruits,
flowers, nuts, or candies.

Tiny Treasure A tiny china cup becomes a
most treasured table favor when it is tied onto a
napkin and serves as a napkin ring. Choose a
one-of-a-kind piece that matches the color scheme
of your dinner party and then find matching ribbon
to tie the cup onto the napkin.

Before and After
Dish Display

Find it! Choose sherbet glasses and goblets with fairly flat bottoms to use in this clever centerpiece. Then find plates of at least two sizes to add to the dish combination to create this sparkling centerpiece. Be sure that the dishes feel stable and secure when placing them on top of one another.

Arrange it! Start by inverting the largest goblets leaving ample space between to build a support for the first plate. Add the first plate and then the smaller sherbet glasses inverted on their tops. Next add a smaller plate with the starring dish on the top. Fill with roses, greens, or whatever fits your celebration.

Layer goblets and plates
to make a centerpiece they'll
remember forever.

For more ideas for
making quick compotes,
turn the page.

Party Dishes

A favorite collection, such as this 1950s set of

aluminum dishes can serve a new purpose as a

centerpiece to hold goodies for the guests.

Instead of punch or lemonade, fill the pitcher with

party horns and fill the tumblers with popcorn and

candy. Arrange the pieces on a brightly colored tray

and set in the middle of the table or on the buffet

for some party fun.

Before and After
Feathers and Flowers

Find it! Gather together an unexpected group of items to create this beautiful buffet arrangement. Choose a bean pot or other deep dish and then find accessories in the same colors. We have chosen all black dishes for our arrangement. For the outdoor look we are trying to create, we have added pheasant feathers and sunflower seeds to the mix of materials we need. A small piece of floral foam is the magic that holds the flowers and feathers together.

Arrange it! Start by placing the floral foam in the bottom of the pot. Cut it with a knife if necessary to fit the pot. Add water and let it soak until it has absorbed all the water it can. Cut the sunflowers and place in the water. Add the feathers in the foam. Fill a small dish with sunflower seeds and add a candle to complete the pretty look.

Combine some unexpected items in matching dishes for a clever arrangement.

Reds Together

Look for spectacular dishes all in a similar hue that

you can showcase on a pretty cake plate. These vintage

dishes are called "goofus" glass and were made about

1900. Painted on the outside instead of the inside, the

pieces were very inexpensive when first made, and

have beautiful color and texture. Usually made in red

and gold, we accentuated the dishes with bright red

flower petals floating in just a tiny bit of water.

Before and After
Beautifully Creamy

Find it! Combining dishes all of one color with just the right fabrics makes a stunning centerpiece. Choose dishes from different sets— and even time periods— that all have the same color values. Then select fabrics that reflect the same hues.

Arrange it! Start by layering the fabrics under the dishes. Lay the tray or largest piece on the bottom and then arrange the other pieces with the largest at the back. Fill one of the pieces with a bloom in the same soft hues and you have created a lovely arrangement.

Dishes and florals in the same
hues combine to make a soft and
sweet centerpiece.

Make in Minutes

Dome Alone Showcase some of your favorite dishes by giving them top billing in a dome of their own. The domes are really covered cheese and cake stands that are serving as art displays for these lovely antique dishes. Stack small butter plates, use a cup and saucer, or just display a single yet elegant goblet in a single dome.

Candy Dish A stack of pretty china cups can serve as a most inviting candy dish. Simply stack the saucers first and then add the cups one inside another. Fill the top cup with some favorite sweet candies and set out for every sweet tooth to enjoy.

Candy Dish A stack of pretty china cups can serve as a most inviting candy dish. Simply stack the saucers first and then add the cups one inside another. Fill the top cup with some favorite sweet candies and set out for every sweet tooth to enjoy.

Simple Glossary

Here are some terms that will be helpful to know when you are decorating with dishes.

China:
Porcelain tableware such as dishes, cups, and serving pieces.

Cake Plate:
A plate made of glass or porcelain with a tall base or stem.

Cut Glass:
Clear glass dishes created by having designs cut into the glass using a cutting wheel and then polished.

Depression Glass:
Sets of glass dishes made during the 1930s oftentimes in pastel colors such as green, pink, and yellow.

Pressed Glass:
Clear glass dishes created by pressing the design into the glass while being formed. Also called patterned glass.

Compote:
A bowl made of glass, metal, or porcelain with a base or stem.

Ironstone:
A hard, durable, heavy pottery developed in England during the 19th century.

Enamelware:
Metalware (usually kitchenware) coated with enamel. Often found in bright or swirled colors.

Quick Takes

- It's fun to decorate with dishes, because of their colors and their shapes. Also, because they were used to serve elegant or everyday foods, they give a personal touch to the past.

- Arrange dishes in lots of places — on top of cabinets, in open shelving, on side tables, or behind glass doors.

- Ironstone pitchers in various sizes and colors — or in all one color — are a welcoming touch to a home's décor.

- For displaying dishes, mix pieces that share a palette, such as all red, white and blue, blue and yellow, or pink and green, or a theme such as floral or nautical.

- Take a retro approach, and display Fiestaware in its bold colors. Mix in some 1950s kitsch — where is that Hopalong Cassidy mug anyway?

- Display old cookie jars and stoneware bowls or crocks atop cabinetry in the kitchen.

- From Dutch Delft to Dresden to Cantonware to Meissen, blue and white china has always been popular. Later, it was variations of the English Willow pattern of transferware that caught the public's eye.

- Did you know that china likely was first fired during the Tang Dynasty in China about 600? Europe probably didn't see china until Marco Polo brought some back from Asia in the late 1200s.

- Farmhouse-style enamelware gives a comfortable look to displayed dishes. While blue and white enamelware is a popular collectible, it also comes in red, yellow, white, green and brown, navy blue, cream and green, gray, and fruit patterns.

- Other pieces of kitchenware, such as lemon reamers or footed cake stands, can be used in so many

- Stack dishes of different colors, shapes, and patterns to take to an event as a cookie or candy tray. To keep it from slipping, place a small piece of waffle foam between the dishes.

ways. Serve lemon slices from the lemon reamers and make a candle arrangement on the cake stand.

- Slow down and sip the tea. It's hard to resist the charms of wonderful teacups. They can be made of china, ceramic, glass, or enamel. Display a grouping of them on a tray, ready for some company and a welcoming whistling teakettle.

decorating with books

Softcover, hardcover, old or new, books are part

of our lives in so many ways. No matter what age

we are, books bring us information, make us

laugh, make us cry, and somehow help us connect

to one another. Use beautiful books in your

decorating scheme so everyone can enjoy seeing

your love of books.

Before and After
All in Blue

Find it! Look around your house to find books and other objects in the same color palette. The colors don't have to match, but they should all fall into the same hue. For example, choose books with covers in all shades and tints of blues and greens for a pleasing look. Now gather your books and favorite pieces together.

Arrange it! The periwinkle blue vase in a medium tone gave us a base color to help choose the books in this striking arrangement. The green-tone vintage books were added with the blue patterned books to compliment the stems of the blue delphiniums. We placed the arrangement on a mirrored mantel to maximize the look. Choose books in colors that you love and create your own arrangement.

Don't let dust gather on those beautiful books—use them in your decorating scheme. Choose book covers and spines that compliment your favorite flowers.

Before and After
Kiddie Curtain Tie Backs

Find it! Any little child's book will be the center of attention when it is used as a clever curtain tie back. Choose a book with some vintage appeal or a small scale book that is wonderfully current. Whichever you choose, this book lover's touch is sure to bring a smile.

Arrange it! Cut a piece of ribbon about 3 feet long. Lay the little book face down and place the ribbon on the back. Use paper clips to secure the ribbon on the back, clipping the ribbon at both the top and the bottom of the book. Wrap the ribbon around the curtain and tie in place. Trim the ribbon to the desired length.

ANIMAL
1 2 3

TINY TALES

Whitman

Little books become
best sellers when they
serve as clever curtain
tie backs.

Cowboy Bookends

No matter what books you collect, you can find

bookends that make the display even more

fun. These vintage cowboy and adventure

books from the 1950s and 1960s feel all cozy

stacked up with cowboy boots from a little

cowpoke's closet. Weight the boots with small

bags of rice or sand in the bottom. Then use

the boots to hold things that might come in

handy or add to the display.

Make it Easy

Good Idea Cover those favorite books with unexpected patterned papers for some decorating fun. Use favorite artwork that your little one designed or use old sheet music to cover your books. Enlarge the images or music if necessary to have a piece of paper large enough to cover the book. Then follow the easy steps, opposite, for making your book cover.

Book Shelf Style Simple book covers in eye-catching colors can make ho-hum books become a key decorating centerpiece in your room. Choose books with wide enough spines that, when covered, can be decorated with all kinds of embellishments. Try eyelets, ribbons, stickers, rubber stamps and more. Making book covers is easy. For instructions on making the covers, see opposite. For tips on using eyelets, see page 155.

Paper Book Covers

What you need

- **Large piece of lightweight to medium weight paper (at least 6 inches longer and 1 inch wider than the open book)**
- **Pencil**
- **Yardstick or ruler**
- **Scissors**

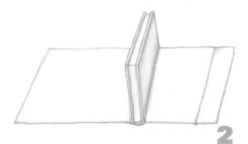

What you do

To trim the paper to exactly fit the height of the book, first lay the paper on a flat surface. Lay the closed book on one end of the paper and use a pencil to mark a dot on the paper at the top and the bottom of the book. Place the book at the other end of the paper and mark the top and bottom again. Use the yardstick and draw a line across the entire length of the paper at the top and bottom markings. Cut along those lines on the large paper.

1. Lay the closed book at the right end of the open paper leaving about 3 inches of paper for the paper flap. Use a pencil to mark a light line at this side of the book.

2. Now roll the book up and stand the book on its spine. Use a pencil to draw a line along the right side of the spine.

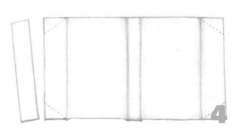

3. Roll the book to the other side and use a pencil to mark a line along the other left side of the spine and the book.

4. Measure about 3 inches or the same distance as the first flap and mark with a pencil. Cut off any excess paper. Using a scoring tool or open scissors, score the lines of the paper. Place the paper book cover on the book. Display your pretty book covered in paper in your favorite decorating spot.

Before and After
Autograph Memories

Find it! Vintage books are always a treasure, but autograph books are a special treat. Not only are they lovely on the outside, but the inside messages bring back visions of a time gone by. Look for these books at antiques stores. Then find a glass tray to display the warm expressions written down so long ago.

Arrange it! Photocopy the inside messages of the pages that you like. Arrange the pages on a flat surface about the same size as the tray. When you like the arrangement, carefully tape the papers to the back side of the tray. Lay the tray on a desk or table and display the original books on top of the tray. Add a fountain pen to the arrangement if you like.

Lovely autograph books of long ago deserve to be displayed both inside and out.

THE NEW
DR. PRICE

What Mrs. Dewey did
with the NEW JELL-O!
48 FASCINATING NEW RECIPES

COCONUT DISHES
That Everybody Loves

Cookbook Jars

Gather up those wonderful old cookbooks and

show them off in large glass jars. (Glass jars

can be purchased at discount and craft stores.)

We used small paperback cookbooks from the

mid-1900s in our center jar and then filled

the jars around it with cookie cutters, shiny

tart molds, and colorful kitchen accessories.

Layer the cookbooks with the smaller ones

around the edges and the larger ones in the

middle. Arrange the jars in groupings of three

or five for impact.

Make in Minutes

Tale Favor A tiny book, either vintage or new, can become a most-cherished table favor when tied to a motif-matching napkin. Use a tiny ribbon to wind around the book and tie to the napkin. Place the napkin and book on top of the plate. Have each guest read and share their special gift with the rest of the party.

Book Smart Let the books you love dictate the colors you choose for accents in a bedroom or family room. Find books that all have the same colors and stack them on top of one another to make a clever statement about your favorite colors and your favorite authors.

decorating with fabric

Bolts of stripes, yards of florals, lengths of

satins—fabrics come in every imaginable color,

pattern, and texture. Whether you are covering a

chair, trimming a window, making a pillow, or

creating a tablecloth, let the glorious features of

fabric make your decorating style say exactly

what you want it to say.

Before and After
Clever Chair Cover-ups

Find it! Most any type of fabric will work to make a cover-up. Fabric with some body or weight works best, but other fabrics can be lined to give them body if needed. Use new fabrics or even vintage or purchased tablecloths to create the look you want for your party or to suit the style of the chair you are covering.

Arrange it! If you are using vintage fabrics, be sure you have enough yardage to cover as many chairs as you want. Take the fabric with you when you purchase the ribbon that will tie at the back of the chair. If you use new fabrics, purchase fabric that has a lot of body or shape to it. For instructions for making the cover-ups, turn the page.

Seat each guest on a chair
decorated with personal flair.
Suit yourself by choosing your
favorite fabrics—ours are made
from 1950s vintage tablecloths.

For more chair cover-up
ideas and instructions for
making them, turn the page.

Make in Minutes

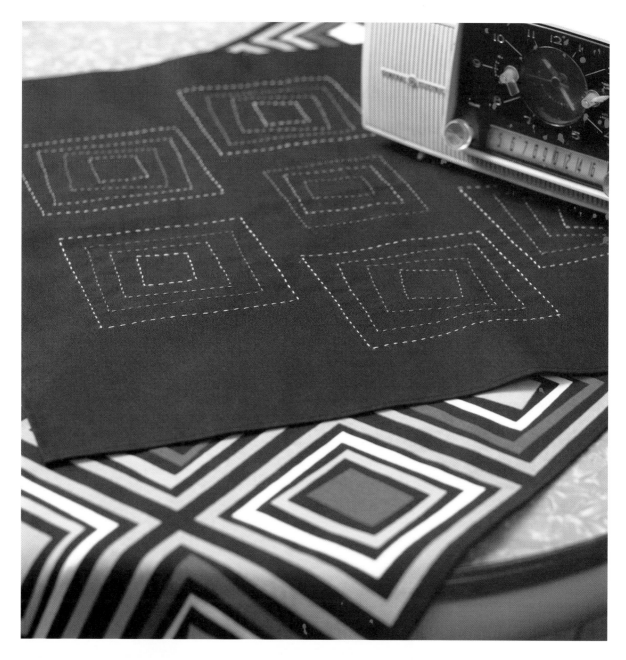

Really Retro   A simple purchased retro print can be the inspiration for a layered look that is perfect for all time. Choose the print that you like and then mimic it by working the running stitch in similar shapes on a plain piece of coordinating fabric. To learn how to do the running stitch, see page 154.

Simply Jeweled Squares of decorator fabric
cut, lined with the same fabric, and layered over a
simple curtain rod, create a simple valance. For a
really stunning look, add a vintage brooch of the
same or different hue to the edge of one of the
layered pieces.

Make it Easy

Good Idea Pretty pillows become even prettier when they are all wrapped up with a polka-dot ribbon. Choose the ribbon that fits your decorating scheme and then tie the ribbon around the pillow just as if you were tying a bow on a package. Trim the ends and toss the pillows wherever they want to go.

Pillow Ties Purchased scarves become the perfect mate for plain-Jane pillows. Dress them up by simply wrapping the scarf around the pillow or try a clever tie that will stand up to every decorating challenge. To learn how to make the tie, see the instructions, opposite.

Pillow Ties

What you need

- **Two purchased long scarves *or* 3 to 4 yards of wide ribbon**
- **Scissors**
- **Purchased pillow**

What you do

The length of the scarves or ribbon you will need depends on the size of the pillow. Each length or piece should be at least 4 times the width of the pillow. If using ribbon, cut the ribbon in half.

1. Using one of the long scarves or one of the pieces of ribbon, wrap the pillow around the middle and make a square knot.

2. Using the other scarf or piece of ribbon, fold that piece back and forth in an accordion fashion.

3. Carefully lay the folded scarf or ribbon on top of the square knot.

4. Use the tails of the square knot to tie another single knot around the folded piece. Tie another knot on top of the single knot and adjust the bow. Trim the ends of the ribbon to the length you like.

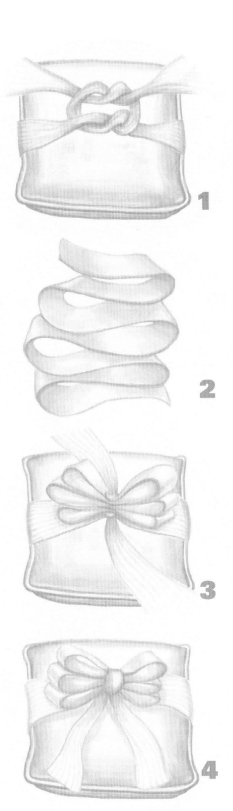

Before and After
Rosette Curtains

Find it! A length of fabric and simple rubber bands are all it takes to make beautiful curtains for any window. Choose light- to medium-weight decorator fabric or yardages of any medium-weight fabric in colors and patterns that suit your room. Large cup hooks hold the rosettes in place.

Arrange it! Decide what length you want your curtains to be. Curtains with rosettes can hang to the floor or stop at mid-length, just dusting the edge of the window sill. Iron the fabric well before you start to remove any fold lines. For more ideas and instructions to make the curtains, turn the page.

A length of fabric and household rubber bands make a stunning window statement in no time.

For more curtain ideas and how to make the rosettes, turn the page.

Make it Easy

Rosette Curtains

If two rosettes make a wonderful look, think what three or more will create! When choosing fabrics for the curtains, an all-over small pattern works well. Stripes and polka dots also make a great window statement. Stay away from very large prints unless the prints can be placed to show when the rosettes are formed.

Common rubber bands work well to hold the rosettes in place but for a child's room try using elastic hair holders. These can oftentimes be found with a colorful bead or other item attached.

Add other embellishments to the curtains for even more fun. Wrap beads that have been strung on a fine wire around the rosette or simply add a tassel that matches the color and feel of the curtain.

Rosette Curtains

What you need

- Fabric in desired length
- Scissors
- Needle and thread to match fabric
- Yardstick
- Straight pins
- Large rubber bands
- Large cup hooks

What you do

Decide on the desired length of the curtain. Measure the width of the window and how far down you have decided each side of the curtain should hang. You can have the curtain hang to the floor or have it any length you wish. Add approximately ½ yard of fabric for each rosette at the window corners. Allow extra yardage of fabric for the slight drape between rosettes. Plan the curtains and rosettes before hemming the curtains. Hem the ends of the fabric (if necessary) after the curtains are planned.

1. Lay the fabric on a long table or on the floor. Bring the long selvage edges of the fabric together. Turn the fabric over so the long unfinished edges are at the back.

2. Mark the middle of the curtains with a pin. From that point use half of the horizontal measurement and measure that amount to each side of the middle. Mark those points with a pin.

3. Bring up extra fabric from the vertical fabric hanging and squeeze it together forming a rosette where each pin is located. Remove the pin and secure with a rubber band. Repeat for the other side. Readjust the rosettes leaving the rubber bands in place.

Place the cup hooks at the window corners. Hang the rubber bands on the cup hooks. Readjust the curtains and rosettes as necessary.

Make in Minutes

Quilt Lovers

Quilters buy fabrics in "fat quarters" or small pieces of fabrics that are precut for making quilts.

Oftentimes these "fat quarters" are sold in groups of fabrics that are all in the same color family or fabric type. Whether you are an avid quilter or just love color and fabric, group these patterned pieces of fabric together by rolling them and placing them in a pretty clear bowl. Add a tumbler full of sewing notions in the center for interest.

Before and After
Fun Bolster Pillows

Find it! Any kind of fabric will work for a bolster pillow, but if you choose a fabric such as fleece or a soft felt, no hemming is required. Try choosing the same type of fabric (such as the fleece we show here) in different colors. Pillow forms are available at crafts and sewing stores.

Arrange it! Making the pillows is so easy that you will want to make dozens for your house and to give as gifts. Because the pillows are simply wrapped and then tied at the end, choose a contrasting color for the pillow tie or pick a colorful ribbon to set off the fabric that you have chosen. For complete instructions for making the pillows, turn the page.

Roll some fun fabric around a
purchased bolster pillow form to
create a soft and lovable pillow
for every room of the house.

For more ideas and
instructions for
making the pillows,
turn the page.

Make it Easy

Easy Bolster Pillows

Purchased towels in matching prints but of different colors work nicely to create fun bolster pillows. The edges of the towels are already hemmed so making the pillows is as easy as can be. See the instructions, opposite, for how to make these easy pillows.

Easy Bolster Pillows

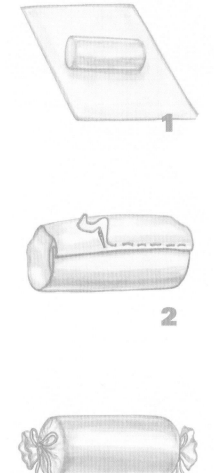

- · Purchased bolster pillow form
- · Pieces of fabric or purchased kitchen towels approximately 20x23 inches or to fit around the pillow form with enough fabric for a 1-inch overlap (fabric that doesn't ravel or prefinished towels work well)
- · Straight pins (optional)
- · Needle and thread
- · Rubber bands (optional)
- · Narrow ribbon or strips of fabric to tie the ends of the fabric

What you do

1. Hem all of the edges of the fabric if necessary. Lay the fabric or towel on a flat surface. Lay the bolster pillow form on top of the fabric.

2. Roll the fabric around the form turning the fabric under about ½ inch where the fabric overlaps. Pin in place if desired. Use a needle and thread and the running stitch (see page 154) to secure the back of the pillow, being careful not to sew the fabric to the pillow. Remove the pins if used.

3. Readjust the pillow if necessary and secure with rubber bands if you like. Then tie the ends using a small piece of ribbon or a strip of fabric. Remove the rubber bands.

Make it Easy

Good Idea Use a soft and pretty cloth napkin to hold a tiny treasure and present it as a gift or a table favor. Lay the tiny gift (such as a piece of jewelry or special wrapped candy) inside the napkin and then fold up and tie. For instructions for making the fun folded napkin, see opposite.

Folded Fabric Fun Bright napkins can become the center of interest in your favorite room when you fold and tie them and then present them with some graphic dishes. Stand the plates on a plate rail or shelf and then stand up pretty folded napkins all in a row to make the look complete. For instructions for folding the napkins, see opposite.

Folded Fabric

What you need

- Purchased napkins or squares of fabric approximately 12x12 inches in desired colors
- Rubber bands (optional)
- Narrow ribbon to match fabrics

What you do

1. Lay the napkin or fabric out flat and accordion fold the entire square. Finger press the creases of the napkin as you fold.

2. Fold the creased napkin in half bringing the ends up.

3. Tie the ribbon or cording around the napkin about 2 inches from the bottom. (Use a rubber band to secure the folds if desired.) Make a square knot and then a bow. Remove the rubber bands if you used them.

4. Pull out the folds at the top of the fabric arranging the fabric as you like.

Simple Glossary

Here are some terms that will be helpful to know when you are decorating with fabric.

Yardage:

The length of fabric purchased. Fabric is usually sold by the yard and comes in varying widths—usually 36, 45, or 60 inches wide.

Seam Allowance:

The width of the seam to be used in the project or piece. Standard seam allowance is ⅝-inch.

Lining:

The fabric that faces the actual piece of fabric. Lining can be made of the same or different fabric.

Batting:

A thick material used to add body to sewing projects such as quilt batting.

Selvage:

The length edge of either side of a piece of manufactured fabric. The edge may include manufacturer's information.

Hem:

The turned-up edge of a piece of fabric to finish the edge and keep it from fraying.

Fraying:

The unraveling of the fibers on the fabric—usually on the cut edges of the fabric.

Valance:

A short length of curtain fabric that usually runs the full length across the top of a window.

Quick Takes

- If you favor tickings or toiles – or both! – you're probably a tactile person. Bring those collected fabrics out of the drawers and boxes and display them in stacks on open shelving.

- Peruse flea markets and tag sales for vintage pillowcases, made special by embroidered patterns and crocheted edging. Wash them and iron them for a crisp, finished look.

- It's pleasing to mix plaids and floral designs, especially if they're in the same color family.

- Cover pillow forms purchased from a fabric or craft store with vintage tea towels. Pick a coordinating fabric for the backing, and mix a variety of pillows on a sofa or window seat.

- Use tea towels to form a simple valance over a curtain rod. Arrange carefully with triangles facing forward, and you won't even have to sew a stitch.

- For a pleasing effect, vary the scale of the fabric patterns you choose. If you have a large plaid fabric, for example, select a medium-scale stripe and a small-scale floral.

- Use small-scale fabrics in a smaller room. Be careful when choosing large patterns. They might overpower a small space, but add a vibrant touch to a larger room.

- Striped fabrics can add width or height to a piece of furniture or to the entire room.

- As for vintage linens, buy what you like. Some dresser scarves, tablecloths, and table napkins are simple, while others have intricate handwork. It's fun to display them and marvel the work that was stitched into them.

- The selvage edge of a fabric prevents the fabric from fraying, Oftentimes it also gives information about the make and designer of the fabric. The color guides used in creating the colors printed on the fabric is sometimes printed on the selvage edge as well.

decorating with frames

There are so many wonderful frames to

purchase—why not use them as focal points

for your decorating scheme? Whether you

paint them, group them, combine them,

sticker them, or just use them as they are

intended, frames can make a statement all

their own and help you make decorating easy

and fun.

Before and After
Happy Frames

Find it! Gather together your favorite scrapbooking supplies to create a wonderful framed piece of art. Choose colorful printed papers, 2-D and 3-D stickers, and other wonderful scrapbooking products. Then get ready for some framing fun.

Arrange it! Start by cutting the scrapbooking paper to fit the inside of the frame. Pick patterns and colors that compliment the purchased frame. Now add stickers and other scrapbooking embellishments that coordinate with the paper in the frames. Use the frame as a table favor or a centerpiece for a special celebration.

happy

lighthearted

joy

Make it Easy

Good Idea Combining two different papers and framing them in a gilded frame can make an art statement all its own. Start by picking papers that have textures and colors that compliment each other. Then fold and frame the papers together. For instructions for folding the paper, see opposite.

Papers for Framing With the beautiful papers and stickers that are available today in scrapbooking and stationery stores, why not frame these beauties and use them in your decorating scheme? Frame them as they are or fold them for some added texture and interest. See the instructions, opposite, to learn how to fold the papers.

Folded Paper for Framing

What you need
- **Piece of art or scrapbook paper at least twice as long as the length of the area to be framed**
- **Pencil**
- **Ruler**
- **Scissors**
- **Crafts glue suitable for paper**

What you do
1. Measure the opening of the frame that you are using. Cut the paper ¼-inch wider and at least 2 times longer than the height of the frame. Lay the piece of paper on a flat surface. Decide how wide you want the folds of the paper to be and mark a dot on both sides of the paper indicating that length. Connect *every other* set of dots with a fine pencil line.

2. Fold on the fine pencil line bringing it up to the next pencil line. Continue folding until you have the number of folds that you like.

3. Using just a tiny dot of crafts glue, place the glue between the folds along each edge of the paper.

4. Finger press the finished folded paper and allow to dry. Frame the paper.

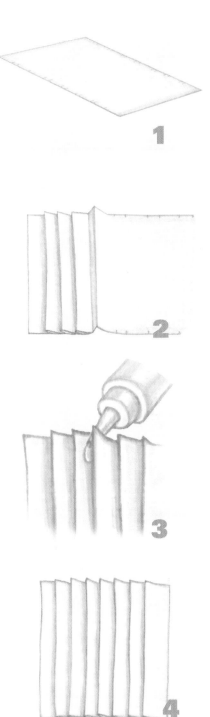

Before and After
Memories in Silver

Find it! Dig out those favorite silver service pieces and group them with some family heirlooms to create a memorable centerpiece. Choose all silver, copper, gold, or pewter pieces and then find frames that match the metal hue. Finally, gather up the wonderful pictures that you want to display.

Arrange it! Photocopy and change the size of the photos to fit the frames if it is necessary and then frame the photos simply. Fold a special hankie or other fabric piece and frame it to add to the nostalgic look. Add tiny flowers in one of the smaller pieces and arrange all of the pieces on a silver tray to reflect your lovely nostalgic centerpiece.

Polish up that vintage silver service and add your favorite silver frames to create a lovely decorating statement.

Before and After
Tasseled Frames

Arrange it! Photocopy the original black and white photos if you like. Colored photos can be copied to black and white as well. Crop the photos and frame the black and white photos in the frames. Arrange the frames on a table or dresser and tie or loop the tassels on the corners of the frames.

Find it! Black and white can make a statement like no other. Choose black and white frames and your favorite black and white photos. Tassels come in all sizes, shapes, and colors. Purchase several in all sizes and shapes.

A simple tassel adds
just the right touch to
black and white photos
and frames.

Make in Minutes

Color Match

Frames of all sizes and shapes look like they belong as a set when they are painted the same color. When purchased, these picture frames were silver, gold, black, and red. But with a little spray paint, they are all part of the same family. Use a spray paint that is suitable for metal or wood, then group the frames with a vase or other item to complete the display.

Candle Holders

Simple frames can double as clever candle holders

with just a little imagination. Frame a piece of

colored paper or fabric in the frame, matching or

coordinating with the candle that will be used.

Frames with glass work best. Take out the stand in

the back of the frame so the frame will set on the

surface. Place the candle on the framed piece.

Simple Glossary

Here are some terms that will be helpful to know when you are decorating with frames.

Gilded:

Frames that are painted with a gold paint or rubbed with a gold paint mixture to give a metallic look.

Mat:

The heavyweight paper frame that oftentimes surrounds a photo or picture inside the frame.

Convex:

Curved glass cover that is sometimes used inside an oval or round picture frame.

Crafts Knife:

A sharp razor-edged tool used for cutting mats and other papers.

Spray Adhesive:

A spray glue that works well for securing photos or pictures to be framed.

Collage:

A grouping of photos or pictures that create a new composition to be framed or used as a decorative piece.

Crop:

To cut the edges from a photo or picture to establish a better composition for framing.

Focal Point:

The main point of interest in a picture, photo, or other composition.

Quick Takes

- Picture frames come in various sizes – 2x3, 4x6, 5x7, 8x10, 11x14, and long ones made specifically for panoramic photos that some cameras take. Plus, there are ornate ovals, just right for vintage photos, and a variety of custom frames – for soccer players, pet lovers, birthday boys, and ballerina girls. You name it, there's probably a specialty frame for it.

- Photos, particularly color ones, are susceptible to sunlight's glare. It's wise to make multiple copies and store duplicates in a cool, dark place.

- Traditional frames often are wood with some embellishment, such as ornate carving details. Modern-style frames usually are metal or simple wood, usually quite thin. Let the photo or artwork determine the frame style. Vintage photos might be able to handle ornate frames.

- It makes good sense to store negatives and photos in separate locations. If the photographs are destroyed, the negatives are available for making new prints.

- Label carefully. Don't write on the front of photographs. Label the back lightly with a soft-lead pencil or with a permanent marker. Identify the subjects, the date, and the event or occasion.

- It's fun to collect vintage photos or albums at tag sales and flea markets. Consider that, even though you likely don't know the subjects, at least you are preserving the photos.

- Don't let a colorful mat overwhelm the artwork. Neutral mats usually work best.

- Consider framing tiny yet interesting 2-dimensional items such as postage stamps or intricate stickers. Leave a large mat around the item for a dramatic effect.

- For a very dramatic effect, copy favorite postcards or other photos or pieces of memorabilia in black and white and then frame them as a collage in black frames.

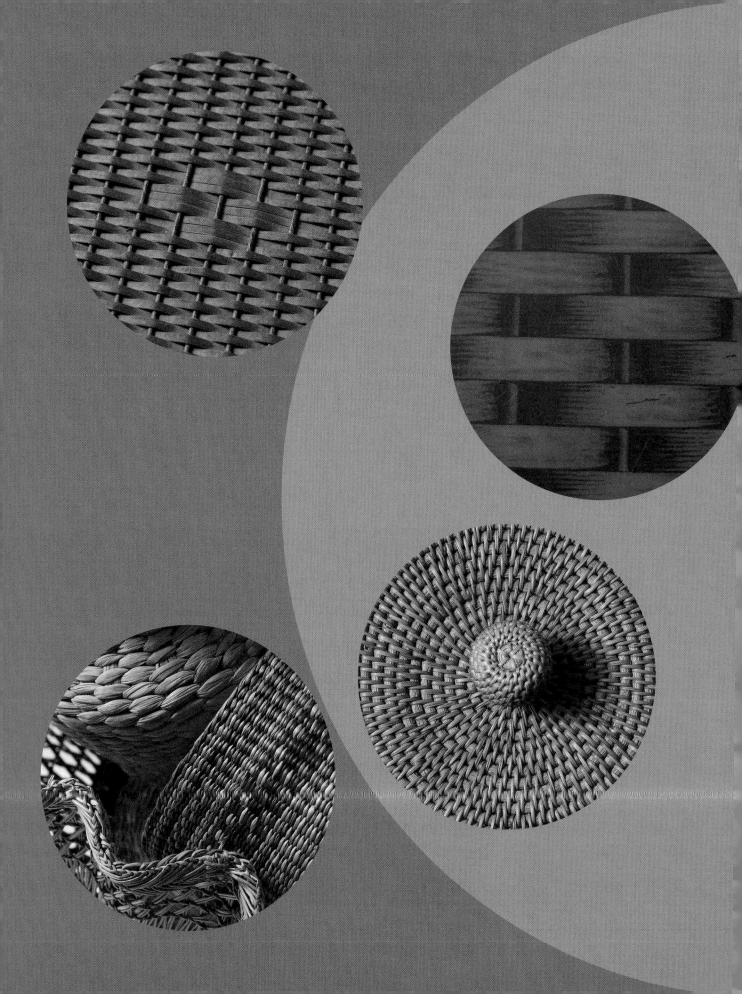

decorating with
baskets

Whether it is a woven traditional basket, an

antique sewing basket, a vintage picnic basket, a

lovely glass basket, a tin painted basket, or a

basket of any kind at all—baskets carry the magic

of having unique sizes, shapes, and textures and

still offer us the luxury of holding a vast variety

of things. Make use of wonderful baskets of all

kinds in your decorating style.

Make In Minutes

Vintage Collection
Grouping favorite baskets makes a clever decorating statement that anyone can accomplish and can provide storage for favorite projects. Let the baskets hold knitting, sewing supplies, or any other favorite items that are pretty to look at and right at hand.

Picnic Table Create a unique end table using stacked picnic baskets. Choose vintage or new picnic baskets that have flat tops and handles that will collapse to the side. The baskets don't have to match in size or design—any combination will bring memories of outdoor fun.

Make it Easy

Basket of Beaded Towel Wraps

Use a simple square-shaped basket to hold brightly colored towels that have been wrapped with inexpensive strings of colorful beads. Roll or fold the towels and wrap them with the beads or tie them leaving a decorative loop. See the instructions, opposite, for how to tie the beaded strands.

Beaded Towel Wraps

What you need

- Towels—bath, hand, fingertip, and/or washcloths
- Large rubber bands
- Inexpensive strands of beads (available at crafts and discount stores)
- Large square-shaped basket

What you do

Lay the towel out flat and tightly fold or roll it as you wish. You can also roll two colors of washcloths or fingertip towels together. Secure with a rubber band.

1. Choose the beaded strand that compliments the towel that you have chosen. Open up the bead strand and place it under the towel. Criss-cross the strand in the middle pulling the loop up at the top.

2. Pull the loop over where it is crossed and up and under the horizontal beads.

3. Twist the top loop around itself at least three times.

4. Wrap it around the horizontal beads and let it hang down as a decorative loop. Adjust the towel as necessary and carefully snip the rubber band to remove it.

Arrange the towels in the square basket with the largest ones in the back and smaller in front or as you like. Place on the floor in a guest room or bathroom for a touch of color and a welcoming look.

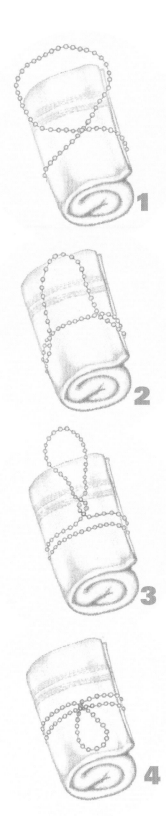

Guest Basket Surprise a special guest with a basket filled with lovely things to be used while staying in your welcoming home. Start with a medium-sized woven basket and fill it with hand-embroidered fingertip towels, scented soaps, lotions, and a few flowers that have been kept fresh in floral tubes.

Silver and Shells Combining the unexpected sometimes leads to a most beautiful arrangement. Elegant silver baskets seem pleased to hold nature's elegant shells. Adding a lovely shell painting on the wall behind the arrangement makes the look complete.

Two in One Nestle one basket inside another
one and fill each with something unique. Our outside
large basket holds vintage magazines—still fun to read.
The inside basket is a container for pretty pumpkins
and gourds. Together they make a wonderful
combination of baskets and colors.

Layered Baskets Wire baskets can be found at discount and kitchen stores and can hold all kinds of things. But for a clever display, layer the baskets first before adding the goodies on the table. Stand up a small basket inside a larger basket to make a background for the arrangement.

Before and After
Flower Basket

Find it! A narrow basket with a handle works best for this decorating project. Choose flowers that are in pots, such as geraniums or pansies. Find some plastic containers, such as disposable plastic drinking glasses, that fit into the basket that you have found.

Arrange it! Remove the plants from their original containers and repot them in the disposable plastic glasses that fit into the basket. Be sure that the dirt is firmly packed into the new container. Carefully set each of the potted plants in the basket. Hang the basket on a hook or doorknob. The plants will continue to need watering but will last for weeks.

Plant your spring plants
in a woven basket and then
present them at the door
for all to enjoy.

Tiny Jewel Holders Tiny china and ceramic baskets make perfect jewelry holders on a shelf or dresser. These tiny baskets were found at flea markets. But whether it is old or new, the baskets will safely hold your tiny treasures.

Make In Minutes

Picnic Fun Let that favorite tree become part of the picnic fun by hanging baskets full of picnic goodies in the tree. Fill each basket with things that you'll need for your picnic party. Find a branch for each basket and use the tree to hold the goodies until it is time for lunch.

Vintage Planters Patterned metal baskets
from the 1950s and 1960s make perfect planters for
inside and out. Place the plant in another container
before setting it in the metal basket to avoid rust on
the vintage pieces. Stack the baskets inside or out.

Simple Glossary

Here are some terms that will be helpful to know when you are decorating with baskets.

Basket Weave:

A textile weave resembling the checkered pattern of a basket.

Bail:

The arched handle of the basket.

Straw:

The natural material of which many baskets are made.

Splint Baskets:

Baskets made from thin strips of wood woven together forming a flatter edge basket.

Hinges:

On tin baskets, the metal piece that attaches the bail of the basket to the basket container, allowing the bail to move up and down.

Coil Baskets:

Baskets that are constructed using a coil that begins at the basket base with material woven through the coil.

Glass Baskets:

Very popular in the early 1900s, glass baskets were manufactured by many leading glass companies as novelty pieces.

Plait:

To interweave the strands of any material forming a braid or basket.

Quick Takes

- Making baskets is often called our nation's oldest indigenous craft. Basketry in this country started with the American Indians, who used whatever they could find— roots, plant stems, bark, and grasses—to make containers for gathering food and storing household items.

- Because old baskets darken and become brittle with age, they need to be "fed". Many antiques dealers recommend sponging off baskets with a small amount of mild detergent and water.

- Displaying a large basket collection can be tricky. A grouping shows off the intricate texture and weaving. In a kitchen or family room, hang them from ceiling beams.

- Hang splint baskets flat against the wall on centered nails for full impact. They can serve as shadow boxes for displaying small items and other mementoes.

- Display variously sized baskets on meat or pot hooks overhead.

- Large baskets can handle being displayed on a shelf placed high around a room or on a bookshelf to break up a row of books.

- Certain baskets give a hint as to their origins. Rye straw baskets often were made in areas such as North Carolina and Pennsylvania. Sawgrass or coil baskets are popular in the South.

- Nantucket lightship baskets are tightly woven, have distinctive designs and are made on round or oval molds. Often the various descending sizes are nested, one inside the other. Generally, they show off groups of eight, with the smallest one being a pint size, up to the largest, which is the 12-quart size. Some newer ones have lids decorated with ivory carvings and are used as purses.

- Faux baskets made of tin were popular in the 1950s and 1960s. These tin containers were painted with a basketweave design to imitate woven straw baskets.

- Prized Shaker baskets, made of woven wheat and rye straw, sometimes have stamps saying "Shaker," "Pleasant Hill," or "Sabbathday Lake", indicating a Shaker settlement.

- Use a large basket to corral magazines or seasonal catalogs in one spot. A recent trend is built-in basket drawers for kitchen or baby room storage.

decorating with
candles

They bring warmth, solitude, color, and mood

to every room of the house. Whether you

prefer stately pillars, romantic votives, tiny tea

lights, simple tapers, or floating candles— feel

the glow by choosing candles to accentuate any

decorating scheme.

Icy Candle Display. Fill a terra-cotta or
ceramic bowl with purchased acrylic chips. Then add a
few simple blue ornaments to complete the look.
To make the look more spring-like, choose candles
and ornaments in pastels or pretty spring colors.

Color Ring Make your own candle ring by placing acrylic flowers and faux sugar grapes into a purchased foam wreath form. Spray paint the individual parts of the wreath in the same color family as the center candle for a beautifully stunning monochromatic look.

Make in Minutes

Citrus Candle

Choose a small floating candle and a small dish in citrus colors such as yellow, orange, or lime green. Fill the dish with water and float the candle. Add a dash of glitter, and place the dish on a larger saucer. Fill the saucer with slices of citrus fruit surrounding the glittering candle.

Candy Stripe Candles come in all kinds of colors and designs. These striped candles are a perfect match for the colors of the candy that surround them. Find a shallow dish and fill it with small candies such as jelly beans that compliment the candles that you have or the colors that you love.

141

Before and After
Dress-Up Candles

Find it! Look around for necklaces and bracelets that may have been forgotten in the jewelry box and give them new life surrounding simple candles. Look for colors and styles that match the candles that you have chosen. Be sure to purchase candles that have a large enough diameter to hold the jewelry.

Arrange it! Try the bracelets around various candles to see which ones you like. The bracelets easily slip over the top of the candles and the necklaces can be wrapped around the candles more than one time to achieve the desired effect. Arrange the finished wrapped candles on a glass plate or tray and place the plate on a colorful tablecloth for a dressed-up centerpiece.

Encircle pretty candles with
simple bracelets to make them
feel dressed up and decorated.

Make it Easy

Good Idea Use a small rubber stamp to stamp a solid-colored candle and then use some gold paint to add texture and color to the stamped piece. Use your finger or a sponge to apply the paint all over the candle. To learn how to stamp the candles, see opposite.

Stamped Candles Combining rubber stamps and pretty-colored candles makes for a clever and unexpected decorating look. Use a touch of gold paint to accentuate just the stamped motifs for a little extra sparkle. To learn how to stamp the candles, see opposite.

Stamped Candles

What you need

- **Purchased plain-colored candles**
- **Flat marbles or buttons**
- **Pencil**
- **Rubber stamps with small designs**
- **Hair dryer**
- **Gold acrylic paint**
- **Disposable paint**
- **Soft cloth**

What you do

To keep the candle from rolling, place a flat marble or a button on each side of the candle on a flat surface. Plan the design of your candle by making a light mark with the pencil where you want the designs to be.

1. Use the hair dryer to warm up one side of the candle. This will only take a few seconds.

2. Immediately press the design into the warm wax. You will need to work quickly. Let the candle set for minute for the design to set into the wax. Continue to warm the wax and then press the rubber stamp into the candle where you want the designs to be. Let the candle completely cool down when all the designs are in place.

3. Put a little paint on the disposable plate. Use your finger as the paintbrush and rub the paint into the design or all over the candle is you like. Wipe off the candle with a soft cloth. Allow to dry thoroughly before using. Never leave a burning candle unattended.

Before and After
Sand Candles

Find it! Colored sand, pretty candles, and chunky glass votive holders make a striking way to decorate with candles. Choose the colors of sand that fit your decorating scheme. Colored sand is available at crafts and discount stores in wonderful colors. Choose a candle that coordinates with the sand.

Arrange it! Start by adding a layer of sand in the bottom of the glass votive. Place the candle in the sand and then continue to layer the colors of sand as you like. Make a paper funnel if that will help you to control how you want the sand to look. (For a paper funnel pattern, see page 156.) Add sand until you reach the top of the votive and you like the look that the sand has created.

Layers of colored sand hold
pretty votives in a simple
arrangement.

Beaded Beauties
Pretty beads, a flat-topped votive holder, and some strong crafts adhesive can make a pretty little candle holder in no time. Choose beads that have one flat side and glue them around the edge of the holder. Allow the glue to dry thoroughly before using. What a pretty little holder you have made.

Candle Float Floating candles come in all kinds of shapes and sizes and are available at crafts, discount, and gift stores. Choose a candle that will float nicely in a goblet or wide-topped stemmed container. Add a pinch of glitter if you like and use as an individual centerpiece on an elegant table.

Candles in a Row

Greet your guests to a row of burning candles to warm

their welcome. A ledge or long shelf is the perfect

place to create this clever look. Use mismatched glass

containers and fill them half full with unpopped

popcorn. Nestle the candles directly in the popcorn,

or place in another glass holder and place in the

popcorn kernels. Line up the candles and wrap some

berries around the containers.

Simple Glossary

Here are some terms that will be helpful to know when you are decorating with candles.

Tealight Candle:

A small, flat candle with a metal bottom used in glass containers.

Votive Candle:

A small candle about 2 inches tall that comes in a variety of colors.

Candle Wax:

Any type of wax that can be used to make candles. Usually comes in a large block or cube.

Taper:

Long, tall candles about 1-inch in diameter that comes in a large variety of colors.

Beeswax:

A honey-colored wax from a beehive. This wax can be used in candles but is often used in creating batik fabric.

Wick:

The center "string" of a candle that can be braided or have metal inside. The part of the candle that is lit.

Candlestick:

Any glass, metal, or other material that is formed into a tall holder for a candle—usually for taper candles.

Candle Ring:

A decorative ring that surrounds a large candle. Often the ring has flowers or greens on it.

Quick Takes

- Candles aren't just for birthdays, special dinners, and religious observances. They can add a warm glow anytime.

- Safety tip: Never place candles near a window or leave a burning candle unattended. Keep children and pets away from lit candles.

- Group mixtures of candles together for more visual impact. Combine candles in one color family – even if their shapes and the shapes of the candleholders don't match. It will be a lovely display even when the candles aren't lit.

- Fill a crystal or glass fruit bowl with water. Add some floating candles. Or, for an individual "glow" at the table, add one small floating candle to a goblet filled with water at each place setting.

- In the off-season for your fireplace, fill the opening with candles at varying heights to create the look of a flame.

- If you're using candles at the dinner table, it's best to use unscented ones. Otherwise, the candle's scent might interfere with the aroma of the food being served.

- At tag sales and flea markets, look for interesting glass candleholders. Then arrange them in a grouping with tapers for an interesting focal point.

- Turn ordinary household items into candleholders. Put sand in canning jars, muffin tins, or small stoneware bowls to hold votive candles in place.

- All candles are made of wax, but beeswax/honeycomb candles are candles that are made from wax that has been shaped with a honeycomb texture. The wax may be beeswax or it can be formed using regular candle wax.

Basic Stitches

Outline Stitch

The outline stitch is used as a decorative stitch to embroider or outline a certain design or motif. Work the outline stitch on the design or line that you have drawn on the fabric or on the printed line or design that has been preprinted on the fabric.

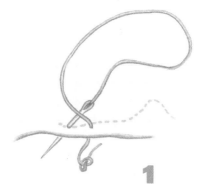

1

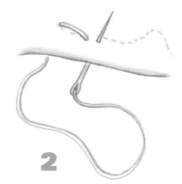

2

1. Thread the needle and tie a knot in the yarn, floss, or thread on one end. Put the needle up through the fabric from the underside of the fabric. Bring the needle back down about ¼-inch from where the needle came up.

2. Bring the needle under the stitch and back up and to the right of where the needle went in about ⅛-inch from that spot.

3. Bring the needle back down next to the first stitch making a line of stitching.

4. Continue making stitches side by side forming an outline of the design. When finished, make a few tiny stitches on the wrong side of the fabric securing the thread. Trim the excess thread.

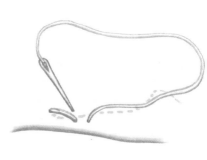

3

4

Running Stitch

Start with the knot on the back side. Pull the needle up through the fabric, and then back down again keeping the stitches about ¼-inch apart. When you are done working the stitch, secure the end by taking a few tiny stitches over each other in the same place. Trim the excess thread.

Attaching Eyelets

Attaching Eyelets

Eyelets can be used on paper projects such as scrapbooking or even on some firm fabric for decoration or to make finished holes for threading cord or ribbon. Eyelet tools are necessary for making the eyelets, and are available at crafts and scrapbooking stores.

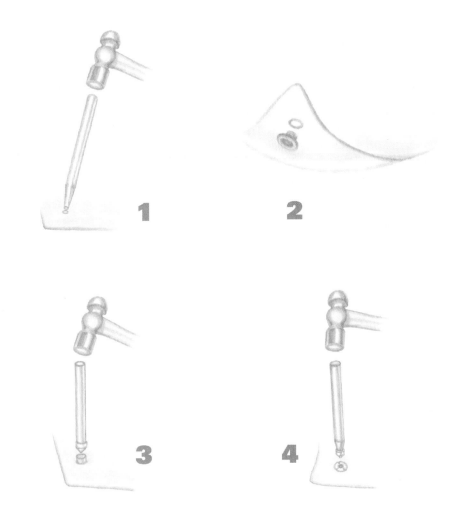

1 Decide where you want the eyelet to be and make a small dot with a pencil. Use the eyelet hole maker and a hammer to make a hole in the paper or fabric where you made the dot with the pencil.

2 Push the eyelet into the hole from the back side with the right side down and the prong part up.

3 Using the eyelet spreader tool and a hammer, center the tool and hit with the hammer, spreading the metal on the eyelet into the paper or fabric.

4 Repeat hitting the tool with the hammer one more time to secure the eyelet in place.

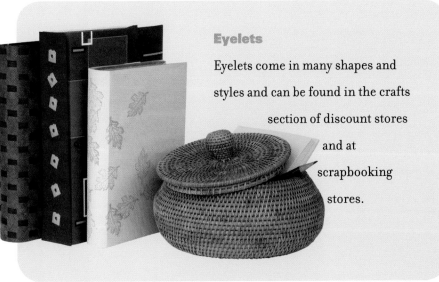

Eyelets

Eyelets come in many shapes and styles and can be found in the crafts section of discount stores and at scrapbooking stores.

Funnel Pattern

Overlap

To make funnel, trace pattern and draw around pattern onto lightweight paper marking all lines. Form the paper into a cone shape matching up the overlap on the pattern. Glue or staple to hold in place.

Sources

Glitter
The Art Institute
www.artglitter.com

Floss
DMC
Port Kearney Building 10
South Kearney, NJ
07032-0650

Ribbon
C.M. Offray & Sons
(800) 344-5533

Scrapbooking Papers and Eyelets
EK Success, P.O. Box 1141
Clifton, NJ 07014-1141
(800) 524-1349
www.eksuccess.com

Yarn
Coats
P.O. Box 1530
Albany, GA 31703
PHONE (800) 445-1173
FAX (229)430-7427
www.modadea.com

Acknowledgements

Lyne Neymeyer (book design)

Lyne has designed dozens of books for various leading publishers across the country. She also teaches book design at the university level and brings a fresh and creative approach to every book she designs. A photographer as well as a designer, Lyne's talents are many as evidenced in the amazing and varied styles she is able to create in any and all of her design and photography work.

Kristen Krumhardt (illustrator)

With a degree in biological/premedical illustration, Kristen has a special talent of being able to draw what she sees with incredible accuracy. Also an avid crafter and talented artist, Kristen brings a fresh and beautiful approach to her precise drawings making them a delight to look at.

Dean Tanner (photographer)

A talented food and crafts photographer, Dean Tanner of Primary Image is best known for having a great eye for composition and color in his work. His work can be seen in various books and magazines across the country including Better Homes and Gardens® Crafts magazines and Cuisine® magazine.

Pete Krumhardt (photographer)

Known across the country and the world for his beautiful photography, Pete is best known for his understanding of light and his work with gardens and nature. His work can be seen in numerous publications including Better Homes and Gardens® books and magazines.

Index

ABOUT THE AUTHOR

Carol Field Dahlstrom has produced over 75 crafts, food, decorating, children's, and holiday books for Better Homes and Gardens®, Bookspan®, and from her own publishing company, Brave Ink Press. She has made numerous television, radio, and speaking appearances sharing her books and encouraging simple and productive ways to spend family time together. Her creative vision and experience make her books fun as well as informative. She lives with her family in the country near Des Moines, Iowa, where she writes and designs from her studio.

Also from Brave Ink Press

If you liked this book, look for other books from Brave Ink Press:
- Simply Christmas
- Christmas—Make it Sparkle
- Beautiful Christmas
- An Ornament a Day
- College Kids Cook
- Cool Crafts to Make—even if you don't have a creative bone in your body!
- Christmas Together
- The Little Book of Christmas Alphabets

To order books visit us at www.braveink.com

Brave Ink Press—the "I can do that!" books™